ANALYSIS

Going Nuclear

The influence of history and hindsight on the Iranian nuclear negotiations

Ozzie Paez

FORT COLLINS, CO/USA

Decisions to Lead
Fort Collins, CO
USA
www.ozziepaezresearch.com

Book Layout © 2014 BookDesignTemplates.com
CreateSpace Publishers

Going Nuclear/Ozzie Paez. -- 1st ed.
ISBN 978-1533469250

To my father, who risked and sacrificed so much in the service of freedom, country and family—and to my daughter, who makes it all worthwhile

There never will be dependable correlation between the intensity of the interaction and the quality of the product.
—THINKING AND WRITING *by Robert S. Sinclair*

CONTENTS

{ i }

Preface

Mastering decision making requires that we study the strategies and methods employed by decision makers in different contexts. It's also important to learn about barriers to clear thinking and objective analysis, which include a variety of fallacies and biases that individually and collectively can blind, influence and confound us. Hindsight bias is among the most common and pervasive of these because it affects how we remember the past, understand the present and foresee the future.

I've previously discussed the influence of hindsight bias in various blog posts focusing on personal and organizational decision making, and in different contexts including banking and finance, crime and terrorism. This book considers its likely influence on leaders and policy makers in Russia, China and the Middle East, as their decisions set the stage for a potential conflict and nuclear arms race in the region. It describes the impact of Russian actions against Ukraine, the implications for other countries threatened by regional neighbors and offers insights into the positions taken by Russian President Vladimir Putin and the Chinese government with regard to Iran's nuclear program.

Why should those of us who are not involved with foreign policy study this case? Because it can help us understand how hindsight and other biases undermine our ability to analyze situations and make effective decisions. We can also learn to spot the influence of these biases in other global contexts important to business, including international trade and finance. Finally, by studying how biases affect leaders on the international stage, we can become more sensitive to their effects on our own thinking and decision making. As I've written in the past, if you are a leader and decision maker, it is a foregone conclusion that you have been, are and will be affected by hindsight and other biases—you cannot avoid it. Fortunately, you can learn to tame their damaging effects.[1]

{ 1 }

Introduction

Violent history is being written once again on the European continent even as Western media focus on the threats and brutal behavior of ISIS in the Middle East. Putin's government, having successfully conquered and annexed Crimea, continues with its policy to further expand Russia's influence, if not outright control, over large areas of eastern Ukraine. What is often missed in discussions of these events is that Russia's behavior would likely have been very different had Ukraine kept at least part of the nuclear arsenal on its territory when the Soviet Union collapsed. That is just the latest lesson to emerge from a not-so-new world order in which countries can effectively defend their borders and interests if they possess a nuke or two—ten, twenty or more, even better. Is it any wonder that nations who feel threatened by more powerful adversaries are seeking to acquire them?

The response from the international community to Iranian efforts to develop and acquire nuclear weapons has been mixed. Western governments in general and the United States in particular have been alarmed at the growing threat of proliferation, concerned that the likelihood of future use will increase as more nations become nuclear powers. By contrast, Russia and China have not been as visibly concerned, at least in Iran's case. Putin's calculus in abetting Iran's nuclear ambitions stands in contrast to Washington's positions at the UN and in recent negotiations. China's more collective leadership[2] similarly appears less concerned and more in line with Russia's position. Are the Russian and Chinese governments being reckless or do they know something the rest of us don't?

One potential explanation is that Russian and Chinese leaders and policy makers are being influenced by hindsight bias, one of the most seductive, difficult to avoid and damaging cognitive traps. This bias, also known as creeping determinism, describes a process whereby our knowledge of actual events influences us to believe that the way things turned out was likely, even predestined, all along. This, in turn, influences how we analyze and integrate information to make sense of the present and construct our perception of the future.[3] Unfortunately, hindsight does not provide foresight, even though we are cognitively predisposed to believe that it does—that's the essence of hindsight's damaging bias.

How can we estimate the influence of hindsight on a particular crisis, negotiation or situation? One way is to consider history, particularly the issues, questions and hypotheses that were considered by affected parties before actual events took place. We can look at previous crises, for example, and the benefits and risks faced by leaders making consequential decisions in the face of uncertainties, and then evaluate their responses and behaviors in the aftermath of their decisions and actual outcomes. What knowns and unknowns were considered? What conclusions and decisions did they make? What were their concerns and expectations at the time decisions were made? How do their original statements and positions compare to later ones, after outcomes were known?

This analytical approach is not new. It goes back at least to the early 1960s and the work of Roberta Wohlstetter at the RAND Corporation. Her research and analysis on the failures of intelligence in the months, weeks and days leading to the attacks on Pearl Harbor focused on how hindsight affected foresight in intelligence analysis.[4] She later applied a similar approach to compare American intelligence failures at

Pearl Harbor with successes during the Cuban Missile Crisis forty years later.[5]

This book employs a similar approach in a longer historical context that takes into account the histories and experiences of two former American adversaries and current competitors: Russia and Communist China. It then considers how the history of nuclear weapons proliferation, use and deterrence are illuminating and biasing other players, including Iran, Israel and the Sunni Arab countries in the region.

Living with Nukes—The Early Years

The world has lived with nuclear weapons for seventy years, during which time they've been used twice in war, in 1945, when the United States dropped the first bomb on Hiroshima and another on Nagasaki three days later, effectively ending the war with Japan. The Soviet Union did not have nuclear capabilities during and immediately after the war, although, unbeknownst to their American allies, its spies had supplied it with blueprints and other technical details of America's nuclear bomb designs. Joseph Stalin did not hesitate in launching a nuclear weapons program, even in the face of numerous technical, political and military risks and uncertainties. And those risks and uncertainties did not evaporate after the Soviet Union exploded its first nuclear bomb in

1949. While having "the bomb" made a statement, it did not give the Soviet Union the capacity to threaten the US mainland. By contrast, America's forward bases in Europe and Asia, along with long-range bombing capabilities, put all of Eastern Europe and large areas of the Soviet Union within reach.

Complicating the international picture in the late 1940s were the deteriorating relations between the one-time allies. US President Harry S. Truman had come to see Stalin not as a partner for peace, but as a power-hungry autocrat intent on controlling the nations his armies occupied after the war. Stalin's heavy-handed installation of communist governments throughout Central and Eastern Europe violated, in Truman's view, the spirit, if not the letter, of the Potsdam agreements. Given Truman's harder line, Stalin could not assume that the US would stand by and allow the Soviet Union to become a nuclear-armed adversary; thus, the Soviet development program and first nuclear bomb test were conducted in secrecy.[6]

The US government was caught off guard by the Soviet nuclear explosion, which was detected using sophisticated methods unknown to the Soviets. American intelligence had predicted a Soviet test no earlier than 1951 and potentially as late as 1953. Stalin was in turn surprised when Truman announced that the Soviets had conducted a nuclear test.[7] He had expected to keep it a secret until the Soviet Union was better prepared to match the American nuclear arsenal and must have wondered how the US would respond now that the Soviet nuclear program was in the open. Would the US accelerate its nuclear research and increase deployment of nuclear weapons in bases surrounding the Soviet Union? Would Truman, who had proved to be less accommodating than his predecessor, Franklin D. Roosevelt, take advantage of America's fleeting nuclear monopoly to enforce Potsdam agreements? At this point, the Soviets had no way to know what the US would do but did know that they were at a power disadvantage.

The American reaction was to continue nuclear research and improve the readiness and reach of its nuclear forces. It began a military-political process that brought Europe under its nuclear umbrella, guaranteeing its security against external aggression from the Soviet Union.[8] But it did not leverage its fading nuclear monopoly to threaten the Soviet position in Central and Eastern Europe by, for example, extracting concessions or demanding compliance with Potsdam. This new knowledge settled questions on the Soviet side, clarified uncertainties and triggered a reassessment of different scenario probabilities. Scenarios that were once considered credible but were contradicted by actual outcomes would have quickly faded from consideration and memory. And even when contemporary documents preserved aspects of the beliefs and positions at play in earlier times, the actual thinking and mindsets involved would have been lost. These are, psychologists and neuroscientists tell us, characteristics of our memory system and hindsight processes, which inevitably bias our perception of the present and foresight of the future.

In Soviet historical memory, proliferation had not led the Americans to use or threaten the use of nuclear weapons to prevent the Soviets from becoming a nuclear power. And becoming a nuclear power had raised its international posture and allowed the Soviet Union to challenge American post-war dominance within a short period of time and at comparatively low costs. These were important considerations for a new empire struggling to repair its economy, while being burdened by the countries it controlled, and being challenged by America's intact capitalist economy. More importantly, Western European economies were recovering much faster than those controlled by Moscow, in part due to massive economic aid provided by America's European Recovery Program, i.e. the Marshall Plan.[9]

In the absence of a nuclear arsenal, the Soviet Union in the post-war years would have been relegated to an old-fashioned, second-rate empire with all the attendant costs of a wannabe superpower and few benefits beyond greater national pride. It would have needed an even larger military to defend the homeland and protect its territorial gains, which in turn would have taxed its poorly performing economy. Instead, nuclear weapons made it economically feasible for Stalin's Soviet Union to retain control of its territorial conquests without potentially going bankrupt. These benefits were recognized by future Soviet governments, which worked to ensure that the Soviet Union never again fell far behind the United States in its nuclear capabilities.

Mao Zedong and his Chinese Communist Party faced similar questions, risks and uncertainties a decade later as they moved to turn China into a nuclear power. Mao's Communists had gained control of mainland China in 1949. A year later, he flew to Moscow to negotiate a treaty with Stalin, which ostensibly established an alliance and mutual assistance pact to promote cooperation in their common struggle against capitalism. The resulting Treaty of Friendship between the two countries papered over many differences, including China's claims on Soviet Manchurian territories, Mongolian independence and recurring border disputes. Mao complained bitterly of Stalin's heavy-handed treatment and lack of respect, which fed mistrust into their relationship from the start. His relationship with Nikita Khrushchev, who succeed Stalin in 1955, proved even more difficult as the two leaders vied for influence and leadership of the socialist world. Tensions grew over differences in their approach to the West as Khrushchev moved toward a coexistence model, while Mao pushed for greater confrontation.[10]

The Soviet Union had promised in the context of their treaty to provide China with blueprints and technical assistance with its nuclear weapons program. Their joint efforts helped China move closer to becoming a nuclear power as an external junior partner to the Soviet's weapons program. The Chinese, who did not want to rely exclusively on Soviet technical support, also established an independent program in the mid-1950s. That program became increasingly important as their relationship with the Soviets quickly deteriorated in the following years.

Khrushchev ultimately pulled Soviet technical advisors out of China in 1958 and reneged on transferring additional nuclear weapons technology. Relations between the Communist giants remained difficult, fed by internecine rivalries and festering border disputes. It was in this environment that China accelerated its own nuclear weapons program and the development of missile delivery systems. Those efforts proved highly successful; in a period of just 38 months, China exploded a nuclear bomb (1964), tested a nuclear-capable missile (1966) and detonated a hydrogen bomb (1967).[11]

Like Stalin and the Soviet government years before, Mao and his government must have pondered what the US and Russia might do in response to its nuclear tests.

The US at the time recognized the government in Formosa (Taiwan) as the legitimate Chinese government and guaranteed its independence against threats from the mainland. The two countries had fought a hot war in Korea and were increasingly embroiled in a new conflict in Vietnam. Tensions between Beijing and Moscow remained high during the late 1950s and early 1960s as a result of their unstable borders, diverging foreign policies and differing national interests. The strain was magnified by the continuing mutual mistrust between Khrushchev and Mao. Would Moscow and Washington, individually or together, move against China or its interests? Would Moscow try to settle border and other disputes before China developed a credible nuclear deterrent?

Mao's China, just like Stalin's Russia, developed and deployed its nuclear arsenal without being overtly threatened or coerced by the existing nuclear powers. And as with the Soviets, nuclear weapons raised China's global power stature and deterred its adversaries. In hindsight, the worst case scenarios did not materialize, while the positive outcomes proved strategically, militarily and politically lasting. Nuclear weapons had, once again, raised a developing country with a poorly performing centrally planned economy to superpower status. This hindsight knowledge would have influenced their foresight and, based on China's reaction to Iranian proliferation efforts, appears to remain influential to this day.

{ 2 }

Biased Costs, Benefits and Implications

The emergence of particular hindsight biases is, much like decision making, a process, not an event. That means that once a biased mind-frame develops, new events will be interpreted from that frame of reference. Russian and Chinese experiences developing and deploying nuclear weapons supported the position that there were limited risks of outside intervention to prevent proliferation, but the question of whether proliferation might lead to the use of nuclear weapons remained unanswered. During the 1950s and early 1960s, US and Soviet policy makers believed that nuclear weapons could be used again in a future war and

15

prepared accordingly. School children in the US, for example, practiced diving under their desks and covering their eyes to protect themselves from imaginary nuclear blasts, while the Soviet Union regularly conducted large scale civil defense exercises.

The US abandoned most of its civil defense drills in the late 1960s as it increasingly embraced the doctrine of Mutually Assured Destruction (MAD). It called for the population centers of both countries to be left essentially unprotected, ostensibly making a nuclear war unthinkable. The Soviet Union, which did not fully embrace MAD, considered effective civil defense an important component of its defense strategy and thus kept developing and practicing increasingly complex scenarios into the 1980s.[12, 13] The two sides held very different views of fighting and surviving a nuclear exchange, and those differences would be reflected in their strategic mindsets throughout the Cold War.

In the meantime, history was recording a string of contentious events, any of which could have led to the use of nuclear weapons but ultimately did not. The US and the Soviet Union had clashed over the Soviet blockade of Berlin in 1948-49, the building of the Berlin Wall in 1961, the Cuban Missile Crisis in 1962, and the threatened Soviet intervention in the Middle East during the 1973 Yom Kippur War. In the latter situation, President Richard Nixon raised the US threat level to the highest peacetime setting, DEFCON III.[14] In each of these cases the US practiced a form a nuclear diplomacy that relied on American nuclear capability to buttress its diplomatic initiatives and deter aggression. Yet American presidents did not transfer the decision to use even tactical nuclear weapons to theater commanders in Europe during the Berlin crisis, nor in Korea during that war. President Truman threatened their use in Korea by moving nuclear weapons and B-36 bombers to the region but did not authorize a nuclear attack.[15]

Beyond US-Soviet relations, China and the Soviet Union repeatedly clashed along their border during the 1960s and reportedly came close to escalating a 1969 dispute into a nuclear exchange; in the end, they stepped back from the brink.[16] Likewise, the Israelis sustained heavy casualties in multiple wars with their Arab neighbors without resorting to using nukes, which, according to US intelligence, Israel had acquired in the mid- to late-1960s.[17] India and Pakistan have similarly avoided using nuclear weapons during recurring conflicts and crises[18], and even the unstable North Korean government has thus far only threatened their use.

Historically, nuclear weapons have a proven record of raising national profiles in international power politics and serving as effective deterrents, but their once-expected use has thus far not materialized. They helped countries like Russia and China offset their relative economic weaknesses by shifting the focus of competition to an area where they could effectively compete and reach parity with their adversaries. Today, nuclear weapons are the only reason an economically and socially failed state, North Korea, matters to regional economic powers outside the Korean Peninsula, i.e. the US and Japan. And, equally important, Russia's ability to intimidate and conquer large areas of a neighboring country, Ukraine, relies in part on it being the only nuclear player in the game.

In the Russian-Chine context, nuclear weapons have in hindsight proven effective at leveling the playing field with adversaries that enjoyed significant economic and technical advantages. They have been essential to the pursuit and protection of national interests, without either country resorting to actual use.

Other countries similarly avoided using nuclear weapons, even when their use would have guaranteed military victory at much lower costs in lives and material. While uncertainties remain, the history of the past seventy years evidently suggests to Russian and Chinese leaders that the risks of nuclear powers using nuclear weapons to settle disputes with adversaries can be practically and effectively managed. It is this hindsight bias that can overly influence foresight, resulting in increasingly unaccounted risks and growing uncertainty.

Implications for Iran

The questions, risks and uncertainties faced by Stalin and Mao as Russia and China pushed to develop nuclear weapons are reminiscent of those facing Iran's leaders today as they pursue their own nuclear weapons program. Like Communist China in the early 1960s, Iran has a regional enemy that is almost certainly a nuclear power, Israel. It also faces a distant adversary with a heavy presence in its neighborhood, the United States. And irrespective of Arab hatred of Israel, Gulf States fear a nuclear-armed Iran, with its aggressive foreign policy, much more than the Jewish state. So a temporary alignment of interests between Israel and its Arab neighbors against Iran is a practical possibility that could facilitate military action. Years of sanctions have weakened the Iranian economy and made head-to-head conflict with its US-backed neighbors impractical. For Iran, as with the Soviet Union and China decades ago, becoming a nuclear power would quickly level the playing field with its traditional adversaries at relatively low costs.

Ali Khamenei, Iran's Supreme Leader, and his government must have considered, as Stalin and Mao likely did, the potential of a preemptive conventional or nuclear response by Iran's adversaries. They must also recognize that, once Iran gains nuclear capabilities, those adversaries will be deterred from threatening the Islamic Republic. Even the United States Navy, which has checked Iranian aggression and protected shipping in the Gulf for over 25 years, will face fundamentally different threat conditions once Iran becomes a nuclear power. The US will no longer be able to challenge the Iranian military without risking escalation and a potential nuclear exchange. In hindsight, when Iranian leaders consider the history of proliferation, international power politics and deterrence, their views of proliferation should generally align with those of Russia and China— they are likely to see manageable risks, lasting security benefits and relatively short-term costs.

Implications for Israel and Sunni Arab States

Russian, Chinese and Iranian views are likely underestimating the risks of Israeli and Arab reaction, along with their willingness to actively prevent Iran from becoming the sole nuclear power in the Gulf. Israel and the Arab states are also influenced by hindsight, but that influence is anchored to different histories and national interests that see the same developments very differently.

Israel's government, with its mindset rooted in Jewish history, the Holocaust, recurring conflicts and continuing threats of violence, is heavily influenced towards perceiving Iran's possession of nuclear weapons as an existential threat. Israel has existed in a very unstable and dangerous neighborhood since its founding, having fought multiple wars of national survival since 1948. Thus it has been Israeli policy for decades to prevent neighboring and regional adversaries from possessing nuclear weapons. And it has been willing to act without notifying Washington or asking for external support in enforcing its proliferation-prevention policy, as illustrated by the 1981 attack on the Iraqi Osirak nuclear reactor[19] and the destruction of a secret Syrian nuclear complex in 2007.[20] As Israeli journalist and military historian Yoaz Hadel once wrote in the Middle East Quarterly:

This preventive counter-proliferation doctrine is rooted in both geostrategic logic and historical memory. A small country the size of New Jersey, with most of its inhabitants concentrated in one central area, Israel is highly vulnerable to nuclear attack. Furthermore, the depth of hostility to Israel in the Muslim Middle East is such that its enemies have been highly disposed to brinksmanship and risk-taking. Given the Jewish people's long history of horrific mass victimization, most

Israelis find it deeply unsettling to face the threat of annihilation again.[21]

Sunni Arab countries that view Shia Islam and ancient Persia as historical enemies and have been watching Iran's aggressive moves in traditionally Sunni Arab lands are also bound to view Iran's pursuit of nuclear weapons as a deadly threat and direct challenge to their leadership of the Muslim world. Saudi Arabia in particular has been clear that growing Iranian power and meddling on the Arabian Peninsula represent unacceptable threats to the Kingdom. Their recent attacks on the Houthis rebels in Yemen, whom they see as Iranian proxies, illustrate that the Kingdom's warnings are not just empty threats.[22]

Efforts by the Saudi government leadership to check Iranian power in the region and their strong statements regarding the unacceptability of Iranian nuclear weapons have sparked Western concerns that Saudi Arabia may move to acquire nuclear weapons from a third party such as Pakistan. The Saudis are believed to have funded parts of Pakistan's nuclear weapons program, which may open the door to acquiring nuclear weapons and technical support.[23] Egypt has also raised concerns, particularly over terrorist groups that receive intelligence, logistics and other support from Iran. It has drawn closer to Saudi Arabia as the two countries see a convergence of interests in stopping Iranian influence from spreading.

While Israeli and Arab views may be reasonable and well based, hindsight bias is predictably intensifying their feelings and their need to respond. For decades, these states have relied on the US for protection, but recent events in Iraq, Syria and North Africa are changing the calculus and increasing their perceived need for deterrence independent of American policy. In a region where the most aggressive regional power, Iran, has been actively seeking a nuclear capability, Russian and Chinese support during the P5+1 (America, France, Britain, China, Russia + Germany) negotiations may unintentionally help build a case for preemption and a regional nuclear arms race.[24, 25, 26]

{ 3 }

The Intractable Problem

How likely are Moscow and Beijing to change their calculus on Iran and proliferation? How probable is it that Iran will give up on becoming a nuclear power? Will Israel and Sunni Arab countries accept a nuclear-armed Iran as the US accepted a nuclear-armed Soviet Union in 1949? Or will they decide to act preemptively to deny Iran a nuclear capability? The answers to these questions will only come with time, as Iran's actions and those of its adversaries are revealed. What we can say at this point is that history and hindsight bias are pulling regional adversaries in opposite directions, increasing risks and uncertainties. And those risks and uncertainties are unlikely to diminish, irrespective of the framework tentatively agreed to in late March 2015 by the P5+1 and Iran.[27]

Preventing nuclear proliferation, war and a regional nuclear arms race will require the key players—Israel, the Sunni Arab states and Iran—to overcome the biases of history and more accurately understand the risks, uncertainties and costs of their positions. How likely is this to happen? Research suggests that attempting to overcome the influence of hindsight and similar biases with awareness and reason alone is impractical. Richard J. Heuer, a scholar who spent years at the US Central Intelligence Agency studying how the human mind processes information, how biases can undermine analysis and what tactics could improve analytic thought processes, describes the challenge this way:

> ...these biases are not only the product of self-interest and lack of objectivity. They are examples of a broader phenomenon that is built into human mental processes and that cannot be overcome by the simple admonition to be more objective... Like optical illusions, cognitive biases remain compelling even after we become aware of them.[28]

Why is overcoming our biases in general and hindsight bias in particular so difficult? One possible explanation offered by Heuer is that when we are exposed to new knowledge that answers previous questions and settles existing hypotheses, we subconsciously recalculate our mental images on the subject: "With the benefit of hindsight, for example, factors previously considered relevant may become irrelevant, and factors previously thought to have little relevance may be seen as determinative."[29]

Hindsight bias is influential and persistent, which makes it a difficult barrier not just for analysts, but for national leaders to overcome. It's unlikely, therefore, that Putin or Communist China's leadership will fully reassess their views of Iran and proliferation absent some dramatic event that runs counter to their existing views and calculus.

The same is true for Iran, Israel and regional Arab governments. Their views of the future are in large part anchored to their past and to the global history of nuclear weapons possession and use. Once hindsight informs and anchors foresight, returning to previous thinking becomes impossible and imagining alternatives to currently accepted views of the future becomes much more difficult. In Heuer's words:

> *After a view has been restructured to assimilate the new information, there is virtually no way to accurately reconstruct the pre-existing mental set. Once the bell has rung, it cannot be unrung. A person may remember his or her previous judgments if not much time has elapsed and the judgments were precisely articulated, but*

apparently people cannot accurately reconstruct their previous thinking. The effort to reconstruct what we previously thought about a given situation, or what we would have thought about it, is inevitably influenced by our current thought patterns. Knowing the outcome of a situation makes it harder to imagine other outcomes that might have been considered. Unfortunately, simply understanding that the mind works in this fashion does little to help overcome the limitation.[30]

Hindsight bias does not work in isolation. It often functions as a gateway to other cognitive traps. For example, hindsight can influence a viewer's frame of reference, which in turn can affect their willingness to take risks.[31] Framing effects are important because in making decisions we first frame the underlying question(s), and research suggests that the framing process is susceptible to influences such as hindsight. Hindsight bias can also influence decision makers into ignoring information contrary to their biased point of view. This confirmation bias is another trap that we cannot overcome just by being aware of its damaging effects. Its presence, in combination with hindsight, was noted by Roberta Wohlstetter in her analysis of the Pearl Harbor attack, in which she described the bias as "a stubborn attachment to existing beliefs."[32, 33] Hindsight can open the door and promote such attachments.

{ 4 }

Lessons in Hindsight

Hindsight bias on its own is not going to trigger a war between Iran and its neighbors in the near future, nor will it make a regional nuclear arms race a foregone conclusion. Its influence, when added to the growing volatility in the region, will make it more difficult for regional leaders, policy makers and analysts to envision potential futures outside of historical facts and historical biases, in a region long plagued by wars, violence and terrorism. The implications extend beyond current negotiations and potential agreements because they suggest that Iranian leaders will continue to see nuclear weapons as the most cost-effective way to deter aggression by Israel, the United States and regional Sunni Arab countries. In addition, becoming an acknowledged or suspected nuclear power would likely raise its global stature and influence with Shia organizations confronting Israel and Sunni Arab governments in the region. The importance of nuclear weapons for Iran is reflected in its willingness to first risk and then endure damaging economic sanctions by repeatedly misleading the IAEA, the UN Security Council and the international community.[34, 35, 36]

Israel and regional Sunni Arab governments are keenly aware of Iran's intentions to acquire nuclear weapons and its proven willingness to violate treaty obligations. This has implications for current negotiations and future agreements between Iran and the P5+1.[37] Whatever frameworks, agreements and treaties are ultimately negotiated, they will not be binding on Iran's regional neighbors, including Israel, Saudi Arabia and Egypt. Israel is already a nuclear power, but the others may decide to match Iran's efforts by becoming threshold nuclear powers.

The effects of hindsight bias are discernible in the positions, policies and actions of Iran, Russia, China and the countries most affected by Tehran's nuclear ambitions: Israel, Sunni Arab nations and even Turkey.[38] History is proving an intractable barrier separating the sides and will likely remain so into the foreseeable future. This has implications in the short term for the potential of military action by Israel and Arab countries to destroy parts of Iran's nuclear infrastructure, and in the longer timeline for the potential of a new nuclear arms race in the region. Dealing with these differences will prove frustrating and potentially ineffective for America and its partners, particularly if Iran's drive to become a nuclear power continues, in spite of promises, commitments and treaty obligations.

How Understanding Hindsight Bias Helps Negotiations

Discussing hindsight bias effects with experts and negotiators sometimes raises the question of whether awareness of its influence makes any difference to those well versed in the issues. In the Iranian nuclear negotiations, for example, experts are keenly aware of the history, culture and interests of the key players, including affected parties watching from the sidelines. In this context, understanding cognitive biases may not appear particularly helpful, in part because experts often believe that their expertise shields them from the influence of such biases.

This common "experts' view" actually highlights the importance of understanding biases and their influence. As experts, we expect to put forth evidence and discuss related implications. We have confidence in the clarity of our thinking, the power of our case and our ability to bring others around to our way of seeing things. What we often miss is how biases in general and hindsight bias in particular make our thinking and that of our adversaries resistive to contrarian information, argument and logic. A contest in which both sides acknowledge that their positions are hypotheses to be clarified, challenged and tested is fundamentally different from one in which both sides are influenced by hindsight into thinking of their positions as axiomatic. And when one side is open to challenges, while the other is convinced that it is correct and reasonable, the resulting dissonance can lead to disappointment, resentment and conflict.

President John F. Kennedy ran into this dynamic in 1961 during his discussions with Soviet Secretary Khrushchev over the future of Berlin. Khrushchev had threatened to end western control over parts of the city, which had been agreed to at the end of World War II. That crisis was later overshadowed by the Cuban Missile Crisis, but at the time it brought the superpowers closer to actual conflict than either side wanted. Kennedy had responded to Khrushchev's belligerent position by reminding him that Berlin's status was guaranteed by NATO and America's nuclear umbrella. The US President used the crisis to request increased defense funding, expand the army and navy, procure more weapons and ammunition, delay the retirement of some bombers and ships, and return others to active duty. He prepared the nation for potential conflict in a July 25, 1961, speech that was broadcast through radio and television; his words reflected American frustrations with the Soviet Secretary's conduct:

> *...We do not intend to abandon our duty to mankind to seek a peaceful solution. As signers of the UN charter, we shall always be prepared to discuss international problems with any and all nations that are willing to talk—and listen— with reason. If they have proposals—not demands—we shall hear them. If they seek genuine understanding—not concessions of our rights—we shall meet with them. We have previously indicated our readiness to remove any actual irritants with West Berlin, but the freedom of that city is not negotiable. We cannot negotiate with those who say "What's mine is mine, and what's yours is negotiable." But we are willing to consider any arrangement or treaty in Germany consistent with the maintenance of peace and freedom, and with the legitimate security interests of all nations.*[39]

Kennedy's words reflect the expert's perspective that seeks to negotiate an acceptable future based on reasonable exchanges and some accommodation. They also convey frustration that reason and logic ran into a wall of objections and unwillingness to negotiate rationally and in good faith. These results are typical of situations where biases prove largely impervious to reason. Hindsight bias makes it difficult for those affected to imagine alternative futures that, while different, can still contribute to beneficial outcomes.

Negotiating with a party whose position is anchored to history and influenced by hindsight bias requires an approach that takes into account their deep attachment to their views and resistance to logical argument. Success may depend on actions predating the negotiations that prompt opponents to question or reconsider their frames of reference. The important point is that efforts based on presenting a competing, logically stronger case and expecting greater flexibility and reasonableness will likely prove ineffective. Unfortunately, this is an all-too-common strategy when experts' knowledge and hubris lead them to overestimate the influence of their argument and the logical power of their positions. Kennedy ultimately held his ground, forcing Khrushchev to reassess the implications of his position from the perspective of a potential nuclear conflict, which would have brought devastation to the Soviet Union for the second time in a quarter century.

Failures to reach agreements due to an adversary's deep attachments to their position can be leveraged to make future negotiations more fruitful. They can also grow to deepen existing biases and lead to breakdowns in the relationship as one or both sides erroneously assign ill intent to their counterpart. Understanding hindsight bias can help us avoid mistakes in assigning intent to our adversaries, while helping us take steps to mitigate the impact of the bias on our own views and positions. Heuer's words, which are worth restating, can help us put hindsight and other biases in perspective by remembering that "...these biases are not only the product of self-interest and lack of objectivity. They are examples of a broader phenomenon that is built into human mental processes and that cannot be overcome by the simple admonition to be more objective."[40] These reasons alone make the case for understanding and managing the effects of biases in general, and hindsight bias in particular, as part of developing a negotiating strategy.

{ 5 }

Further Reading

While the United States and its Western allies are not immune to the effects of hindsight bias, I've chosen to focus this discussion on the other players in the negotiations because their positions over the years and during the current investigation suggest that hindsight bias has been highly influential. The US is also affected by its own history and experiences, of course, but its evolving position suggests that other factors and biases are the primary influence on President Barack Obama's administration.

The reference section contains a broad list of papers, documents and books to assist readers wishing to explore the many complex issues of this topic in more detail. They were selected to provide a range of views on historical events and technical information. Solutions for dealing with the effects of hindsight and other biases require general awareness as well as targeted, contextual applications of proven methods. While certainly related, these are topics that are best covered more specifically outside of this book.

Upcoming papers that expand on the information in this book will be made available to my readers at no additional charge. They will address options for mitigating the effects of biases, fallacies and cognitive traps. I may provide additional examples and discussions, as well, depending on the success of the current negotiations. *Please register* to receive alerts when new materials are available to supplement the topics covered in this book. Your contact information will not be sold or provided to other parties.

Register Going Nuclear on the author's website to get updates and access to future analysis papers.

ABOUT THE AUTHOR

Ozzie Paez is a researcher, author, engineer and information systems expert whose services focus on helping leaders and decision makers make better use of information. He is the author of ***Decision Making in a Nuclear Middle East – Lessons from the Cold War*** and the upcoming, ***Informed Decision Makers—And Other Myths and Fallacies***. He has spent over 20 years developing information systems, databases and software for business, government and military applications. In the aftermath of 9/11, he brought this experience to the study of decision making within radical movements and terrorist groups. His research into the background of radical Islamist groups, their culture, leadership and belief systems led to new insights into factors and tactics used in recruiting new members and fostering terrorism at home.

Mr. Paez has co-authored a variety of papers on topics such as military assistance to local authorities after 9/11; culture and security in the context of the April 2007 Virginia Tech shootings; and technical subjects related to information systems and software development. He has published dozens of posts about various aspects of decision making on his blog, ozziepaezdecisions.com, and in newsletters. His interest in history and foreign policy were fueled by his memories of growing up in Communist Cuba, where he learned at a young age that even repressive governments, unencumbered by legal or constitutional limits, are often blind to the implications of important events and emerging threats to their power. Mr. Paez is an American citizen and military veteran of the US Air Force.

LinkedIn:
http://www.linkedin.com/in/ozziepaezlinkedin
Author Website and Blog: ozziepaezresearch.com

References

[1] Ozzie Paez, "Hindsight Bias: Tripping Over the Past on the Way to the Future," *Ozzie Paez's Decisions Blog*, February 16, 2012, http://ozziepaezdecisions.com/2012/02/16/hindsight-bias-tripping-over-the-past-on-the-way-to-the-future/.

[2] David M. Lampton, "How China is Ruled: Why It's Getting Harder for Beijing to Govern," *Foreign Affairs*, January/February 2014, http://www.foreignaffairs.com/articles/140344/david-m-lampton/how-china-is-ruled.

[3] Bauth Fischhoff, "Hindsight ≠ Foresight: The Effect of Outcome Knowledge on Judgment Under Uncertainty," *Journal of Experimental Psychology: Human Perception and Performance* (1975): 288-299.

[4] Roberta Wohlstetter, *Pearl Harbor: Warning and Decision* (Stanford University Press, 1962).

[5] Roberta Wohlstetter, "Cuba and Pearl Harbor: Hindsight and Foresight" (RAND Corporation, 1965), http://www.rand.org/content/dam/rand/pubs/research_memoranda/2007/RM4328.pdf.

[6] D.M. Giangreco, and Robert E. Griffin, background on conflict with USSR, from *Airbridge to Berlin: The Berlin Crisis of 1948, its Origins and Aftermath* (Presidio Press, 1988), accessed at http://www.trumanlibrary.org/whistlestop/ BERLIN_A/BOC.HTM.

[7] William Burr, Editor, "U.S. Intelligence and the Detection of the First Soviet Nuclear Test, September 1949," The National Security Archive, Georgetown University, http://nsarchive. gwu.edu/nukevault/ebb286/.

[8] Milestones: 1945-1952, "Atomic Diplomacy," Office of the Historian, US Department of State, accessed April 2015, https://history.state.gov/milestones/1945-1952/atomic.

[9] "History of the Marshall Plan," The George C. Marshall Foundation, accessed April 2015, http://marshallfoundation. org/marshall/the-marshall-plan/history-marshall-plan/.

[10] James G. Hershberg, *The Cold War in Asia*, (Diane Publishing, 1996), 173-176, accessed at https://books.google.com/ books?id=qlNqWJMN_pcC&pg=PA175&lpg=PA175&dq=k hrushchev+does+not+supply+china+with+nuclear+weapons &source=bl&ots=o4l2E6zpIs&sig=Aufk3h3Uc5z4mqFhkd-ZslxV3Z0&hl=en&sa=X&ei=qhUVVeKyB5XjoATkzILQDA &ved=0CCQQ6AEwAQ#v=onepage&q=khrushchev%20 does%20not%20supply%20china%20with%20nuclear%20we

apons&f=false.

[11] Nuclear Weapons, China, Federation of American Scientists, accessed March 19, 2015, http://fas.org/nuke/guide/china/nuke/.

[12] Daniel S. Papp, "Soviet Perception of the Strategic Balance," *Air University Review*, January-February 1981, http://www.airpower.maxwell.af.mil/airchronicles/aureview/1981/jan-feb/papp.htm.

[13] Personal experience and various works of Leon Gouré.

I met Dr. Gouré while working at the University of Miami's Center for Advanced International Studies in 1976-1977. He was Director of Soviet Studies and I was an engineering student with a job making copies and doing whatever was needed by the staff. I was at the Center one morning discussing with a fellow student the issue of nuclear war and what I understood of Soviet intentions, which was rudimentary at best, when Dr. Gouré came in and corrected a number of my misconceptions.

Dr. Gouré took of his valuable time to share his deep knowledge and understanding of Soviet attitudes on nuclear war and civil defense, a subject in which he was considered the leading expert at the time. That he was willing to do so for a few lowly undergrads who were not in the history program speaks loudly of his dedication to impart knowledge and inspiration. He was a professor at heart. I spoke to him often when he came into the copy room and found him always kind and engaging. I was able to read a number of his writings after his fortuitous impromptu lecture, given that part of my job involved copying many of his studies for the Department of Defense.

His skepticism about Soviet attitudes towards the MAD doctrine was encapsulated in a passage from his book *War Survival in Soviet Strategy*, as quoted by *The Washington Post*: "The fundamental Soviet view is that the better the USSR is prepared for war, the greater and more credible is its ability to deter its adversary from risking military confrontation. This is the main reason why Moscow categorically rejects any concept of security based on a balance of 'mutual assured destruction.'" Ref: Joe Holley, "Leon Gouré, 84; Sovietologist and Civil Defense Expert," *Washington Post* obituary, April 5, 2007, http://www.washingtonpost.com/wp-dyn/content/article/2007/04/04/AR2007040402621.html.

I read of Dr. Gouré's passing with sadness in 2007, while researching Soviet civil defense for this piece. I wanted to credit him for expanding my limited knowledge of the subject so many years ago. I'm truly grateful.

[14] Richard Nixon Foundation, "Defcon III," *The New Nixon*,

October 14, 2014, http://blog.nixonfoundation.org/2014/
10/defcon-iii/.

[15] "Atomic Diplomacy," op. cit.

[16] "Sino-Soviet Border Disputes (March 1969)," from
"Nixon's China Game," *American Experience*,
http://www.pbs.org/wgbh/amex/china/peopleevents/
pande06.html.

[17] Nuclear Weapons, Israel, Federation of American
Scientists, accessed March 21, 2015,
http://fas.org/nuke/guide/israel/nuke/.

[18] Rishi Iyengar, "Military Action, Diplomatic Threats
Between India and Pakistan in Kashmir," *Time,* October 10,
2014, http://time.com/3489191/military-action-diplomatic-
threats-between-india-and-pakistan-in-kashmir/.

[19] "1981: Israel Bombs Iraqi Nuclear Reactor," *BBC*, On This
Day, June 7, http://news.bbc.co.uk/onthisday/hi/dates/stories/
june/7/newsid_3014000/3014623.stm.

[20] David E. Sanger, and Mark Mazzetti, "Israel Struck Syrian
Nuclear Project, Analysts Say," *New York Times*, October 14,
2007, http://www.nytimes.com/2007/10/14/washington/
14weapons.html.

[21] Yoaz Hendel, "Iran's Nukes and Israel's Dilemma," *Middle
East Quarterly* 19 (Winter 2012): 31-38,
http://www.meforum.org/3139/iran-nuclear-weapons-israel.

22 Jethro Mullen, "Why is Saudi Arabia Bombing Yemen?," *CNN*, March 26, 2015, http://www.cnn.com/2015/03/26/middleeast/yemen-saudi-arabia-offensive-why-now/.

[23] Ayesha Tanzeem, "Pakistan Has Complicated Nuclear Relationship with Saudi Arabia, Iran," *Voice of America*, April 7, 2015, http://www.voanews.com/content/pakistan-has-complicated-nuclear-relationship-with-saudi-arabia-iran/2710343.html.

[24] John Hannah, "Fear and Loathing in the Kingdom," *Foreign Policy*, November 29, 2013, http://foreignpolicy.com/2013/11/29/fear-and-loathing-in-the-kingdom/.

[25] Richard L. Russell, "Off and Running: The Middle East Nuclear Arms Race," *Joint Forces Quarterly* (3rd Quarter, 2010): 94-99.

[26] David D. Kirkpatrick, "As U.S. and Iran Seek Nuclear Deal, Saudi Arabia Makes Its Own Moves," *New York Times*, March 30, 2015, http://www.nytimes.com/2015/03/31/world/middleeast/saudis-make-own-moves-as-us-and-iran-talk.html?_r=0.

[27] "Statement by the President on the Framework to Prevent Iran from Obtaining a Nuclear Weapon," The White House, Office of the Press Secretary, April 2, 2015, https://www.whitehouse.gov/the-press-office/2015/04/02/statement-president-framework-prevent-iran-obtaining-

nuclear-weapon.

[28] Richards J. Heuer, *The Psychology of Intelligence Analysis*, (Center for the Study of Intelligence, Central Intelligence Agency, 1999), 162, https://www.cia.gov/library/center-for-the-study-of-intelligence/csi-publications/books-and-monographs/psychology-of-intelligence-analysis/PsychofIntelNew.pdf.

[29] Ibid.

[30] Ibid, 163.

[31] Ozzie Paez, "The Great Decision Frame-Up," *Ozzie Paez's Decisions Blog,* November 16, 2011, http://ozziepaezdecisions.com/2011/11/16/the-great-decision-making-frame-up/.

[32] Op. cit., Wohlstetter, Pearl Harbor, pg. 393.

[33] Ozzie Paez, "Forget The Facts—I Know I'm Right," *Ozzie Paez's Decisions Blog*, May 24, 2012, http://ozziepaezdecisions.com/2012/05/24/forget-the-facts-i-know-im-right/.

[34] Benny Avni, "For Its Nuclear Program, Time Is on Iran's Side," *Newsweek*, July 16, 2014, http://www.newsweek.com/2014/07/25/its-nuclear-program-time-irans-side-259196.html.

[35] Jacqueline Shire, and David Albright, "Iran's NPT Violations—Numerous and Possibly On-Going?," The Institute for Science and International Security (ISIS),

September 29, 2006, http://isis-online.org/publications/iran/irannptviolations.pdf.

[36] William Tobey, "Is Iran Already Cheating on a Nuclear Deal?," *Foreign Policy*, December 15, 2014, http://foreignpolicy.com/2014/12/15/is-iran-already-cheating-on-a-nuclear-deal/.

[37] M.S., "Everything You Want To Know About the Iranian Nuclear Deal," *The Economist,* April 5, 2015, http://www.economist.com/blogs/economist-explains/2015/04/economist-explains-3.

[38] "Turkey Denies Nuclear Weapons Accusations," *Middle East Monitor*, September 26, 2014, https://www.middleeastmonitor.com/news/europe/14375-turkey-denies-nuclear-weapons-accusations.

[39] John F. Kennedy, Radio and television report to the American people on the Berlin Crisis, July 25, 1961, John F. Kennedy Presidential Library, http://www.jfklibrary.org/Asset-Viewer/Archives/JFKPOF-035-031.aspx

[40] Op. cit., Heuer, 162.

www.ingramcontent.com/pod-product-compliance
Lightning Source LLC
Chambersburg PA
CBHW071128280526
45787CB00003B/1215